"One of the most poignant and surprising takes on family life since Akhmatova, rooted in lived experience that many share but few have the combination of courage or skills to articulate in poetry, this is the work of a poet at the full measure of her powers, successfully realizing Yeats's goal for his own work, of giving serious study to sex and the dead."

Eddie Vega   Writer, poet, W.B. Yeats Society of New York

"The ancients once said the stars made music which no one can hear – but it is there – real, speaking to our souls. The music of Casey's poetry we can indeed hear. Her poetry sings with honesty, striking at the reader's heart. This is a brave, beautiful body of work. The power of Casey's poems reminded me of what the poet Muriel Rukeyser once said: 'What would happen if one woman told the truth about her life? The world would split open'. Casey's truth confronts us in her poetry, and challenges us to gaze through her eyes. Her poems tell a woman's truth, the truth we all need to listen to, if we want the world to change."

Dr Wendy J Dunn Novelist and poet

About this book

out of emptied cups explores what it means to be human—a consciousness contained within a shell that dictates so much of what our experience of life will be.

Including internationally award-winning and shortlisted pieces, these strongly felt poems interrogate what it means to be a woman in a world where the *female body* still preordains so much for the *person* it contains. Deliberately weaving in and out of, and cross-referencing, each other, these poems reveal multiple perspectives on the same or related narratives.

At times unabashedly political, this book plumbs the poet's own experiences of birth, death, loss, treatment/mistreatment and *place* in the world—as a woman, as an immigrant, as a parent, as a former environment journalist/author depicting the decline of our planet, as a human being questioning our treatment of others based on lines on a map and 'so many lengths/of slick red tape'.

Collectively these poems strive to cross the boundary between body and soul. To be filled to overflowing. Emptied. To be simultaneously half-full, half-empty. To drink deeply of this one precious cup and find meaning in the traces of what remains—"lifting our hearts/out of emptied cups/and away with them/into the heavens".

the arts council
an chomhairle ealaíon

funding
literature
artscouncil.ie

out of emptied cups
anne casey

salmonpoetry
Publishing Irish & International
Poetry Since 1981

Published in 2019 by
Salmon Poetry
Cliffs of Moher, County Clare, Ireland
Website: www.salmonpoetry.com
Email: info@salmonpoetry.com

ISBN 978-1-912561-74-2

Cover Artwork: 'Powder Flower' by Cezary Korsieko, October 9 Arts, Poland –
www.facebook.com/october.nine.works/

Cover Design & Typesetting: *Siobhán Hutson*

Printed in Ireland by Sprint Print

*Salmon Poetry gratefully acknowledges the support of
The Arts Council / An Chomhairle Ealaíon*

for Rory

plus tibi do, plus mihi habeo

Awards and recognition for poems in this book

'if I were to tell you' won 1st Prize in the 2018 Alice Sinclair Memorial Writing Competition (Fellowship of Australian Writers - Lake Macquarie/NSW, Australia).

'whisperings' won 1st Prize in the Henry Lawson Verse & Short Story Competition 2018 – Traditional Verse (Australia).

'Still I Rise' won 3rd Prize in the Women's National Book Association (USA) Sixth Annual Writing Contest 2018.

'Category four' won the Glen Phillips Novice Writer Award 2017 (Australia).

'death in the city' was shortlisted for the Bedford International Writing Competition 2017 (UK).

'All Souls' was Highly Commended in the Fellowship of Australian Writers Queensland Literary Competition 2018.

'scion' received Honorable Mention in the 45th New Millennium Writing Awards 2018 (USA).

'Portrait of a woman walking home', 'you have to be tough to be a man', 'PLEASE DO NOT FEED THE ANIMALS', 'crush', 'for all the #MeToos', 'Dear son' and 'Still I rise' were shortlisted for the Overton Poetry Prize 2018 (UK).

'nothing happens in the burbs' was shortlisted for the Galway University Hospital Arts Trust Poems for Patience Competition 2019 (Ireland).

'sideshow' was shortlisted for the Bangor Forty Words Competition 2019 (Northern Ireland).

'in a sunburnt country' was longlisted for the University of Canberra Vice-Chancellor's International Poetry Prize 2018 (Australia).

'a great mirror', 'cup in hand' and 'All Souls' were finalists in the Summer Literary Series 2018 Fiction & Poetry Contest (Canada).

'All Souls' was longlisted for the Bedford International Writing Competition 2018 (UK).

'final offensive' was Commended in the Bangor Forty Words Competition 2018 (Northern Ireland).

'burnt offerings' was Poem of the Week on HeadStuff arts hub in May 2018 (Ireland).

Foreword

It is rare to find a poet who writes so powerfully, openly and unguardedly of the most horrific things humans have done as well as of life's most exquisite moments of beauty. In *out of emptied cups* Anne Casey captures both these extremes of experience.

So many qualities come together in Anne's poetry: moral fierceness, wry humour, a delicate ability to lay the self open, an enthusiasm for the shape-shifting play of words. From poems charged with the mystery and grace of language, like 'out of a thousand cups' or 'observance', to the humorous familiarity of 'nothing happens in the burbs', from the unflinching grimness of 'in the name of the Almighty' or 'Suffer the little children' to the eloquent note of lamentation in 'None shall sleep' or 'mutation', or the pointed political satire of 'in a sunburnt country', this collection gives us the sustained sense of discovery that is poetry at its best.

—PETER BOYLE

"Glimmerings are what the soul's composed of.
Fogged-up challenges, far conscience-glitters
and hang-dog, half truth earnests of true love.
And a whole late-flooding thaw of ancestors."

SEAMUS HEANEY

Contents

out of a thousand cups

one warm morning when my soul
defies all twenty-one
of its grams
carried away like a whispered prayer
on a sunburst, flimsy-radiant
drifting high on all-but-still air
into green-golden crowns
of softly swaying boughs
to wonder
at the unknowable—
what if
i had first poured forth
into another cup
a different skin
other sex
alternate state
or into a tiny egg
swelling in the soft round belly
of a feathered form
spearing through the clear
blue air of
one warm morning in
some other time

Observance

To stand naked on cold stone
Emptied cups cascading

Past unblinded eyes
As hands and feet are washed

Within a sea concentric circles pooled
As beneath the welling surface

A square of light appears
A window into that other place

Where they have gone before us
And between the here and there

A chasm unfolds, a great grey void
Filled not with dark or light

Not with a weighting
For the passage

For taken or granted
Given or received

Arrival or departure
Gain or loss

But with the infinite possibilities
Of the here and now

if i were to tell you

when sunbeams stream over yellow underbelly
a honeyeater feasting between gilding leaves
i wish i could fly up there to sit for a while away
from the pace and chaos of ordinary things
                                        that is where

when i spy the upturned cup of a ghost-moon plump
in a deep blue pillowed afternoon i think i must call my Mum
though i clasped her hand while she passed such a long time since
as the tide rasped its shallow symphony over our last goodbye
                                        that is where

when i stretch to parting-kiss the soft pink cheek
of my son now twelve towering
over me i feel again the wrench as they pulled
him from my ruptured belly
                                        that is where

when breath of sea sends me sailing back to
this rough hand gentle over mine my weathered
trawler-captain father steering me away from jagged territory
into calmer waters (still) sometimes against my will
                                        that is where

when i smell your neck to
fall again over the handrail of our
romantic balcony landing in the toy-scattered
couch of our reality
                                        that is where

when i tumble on a crumpled butterfly ensnared
once more by that man-boy-man who tore my wings
(never mind i put them back together in time)
on dark days you can still see the scars but on bright ones
                                        that is where

i would tell you
that is where
the light shines through
the strongest

awash

i was the swallow and spit
an irregular grain
ejected too early
from the oyster's belly
parts of me only a little over
half-done
not the ones you'd notice
unless you were looking through
an irradiated plate

seawater still
rises in tides within
the chambers of my breath perhaps
if i'd been left on that rocky shelf
i might never have
emerged from the shell
clinging still to the
illusion of some submerged
labyrinth where my
air-deficient sacs

might drift weightless forever
in that unending blue

heirloom

i never troubled about living or dying
the devil
may care of my younger days
seeing my feet teeter on more than one smoking
ash volcanic edge howling at the blood
red sunrise
eyes always on the horizon
impulse fuelled jumps off mountain tops not
this unwanted text prompt
laying its lead apron on my chest like
a paw-pressing feline testing the steadfastness
of my internal architecture not
this reminder of the flawed material
bequeathed by my female line
miswritten encryption like
the unwritten inscription on
my love's crinkle-browed
self-inspection at each small digression
this faint shadow
passed on from his father
to whom he is sometime brother sometime
stranger or another
and now i am older finding this undeniable
desire to abide for awhile
unbidden gift
handed down
from my
children

Changeling

for Jack

Who is this creature as ethereal as radiance
as mystifying as the Milky Way
staring backwards into time
standing in the frost-bright
grass, you would teach
me about stars

      After we have compared memories of past
      events—you remembering segments that
      elude my squinting through a too
      -fogged lens and I retelling you
      times you cannot recollect—
      how you would sling

            your star-patterned sippy-cup and slug from
            over your shoulder like a pirate in your
            high perch and the mess
            my god, my glorious
            indulgence of you
            first precious

                  intoxicating breath-stealer, like these far-off
                  stars and love and unfathomable
                  beauty, your radiant youth
                  standing aloft in this ice
                  -lit star-field at twelve
                  already dwarfing me

        with all your maths and facts I don't know
        where they all came from or when
        and I am floating in this vast
        unexplored territory, an
        entire constellation of
        you stretching away

infinitely greater than anything I could
have comprehended from that first
small spark telling me you
existed in me and you
gasp *A shooting star*
Yes I breathe

You are

nothing happens in the burbs

we lay in bed talking about nothing
till two came stomping up the stairs
raging on about nothing
one hot on his heels
what did you do to him?
nothing!

after breakfast you put music on
Adele, Luka Bloom, Joe Cocker, Emeli Sandé
they had nothing in common
but us
eleven a.m. on a Saturday
dancing barefoot in the kitchen
pretending there was nothing
going on

i lolled between one and two
while you did nothing in the garden
got two's help to move it to the garage
nothing in the fridge so we cobbled something together
nothing on tv so we watched an expert panel
arguing vehemently about nothing the government
was doing nothing about while we shook our heads
knowing nothing
would change

slouching on the couch
nothing between us
but the dog
eight feet in the air
a howl and crash from upstairs
what happened??!
nothing!! in unison, too quick
what was that all about? nothing at all

we split a cider
yours straight from the bottle
mine from a champagne flute
making an occasion out of nothing
till we went to bed, in no hurry
we had nothing on

and there is nothing, absolutely nothing
i would change

wildness

i feel every pace and turn
crawling beneath the surface of your skin
erupting in tiny jagged twitches
a vein throbs above contracting pupils
muscles flex and relent, yet never relax
the waiting in you thickening through years

one day i know you will burst forth
and sprint away into the
flickering flame of evening
away into the dark forest that
scratches beyond our
blinded windows

and i will curl up
wrap myself in your shed skin
and marvel at its length
its strength
its tenderness
all that had held you back

your wildness denied

heat

f vodka in a long-stemmed cosmo tongue circling maraschino stalk love knotted
between bared teeth burnt orange slicked lips lick bittersweet nothings silk
slipped over easy skin thighs crossing uncrossing recrossing suggesting
an undressing pounding pulse rush of unintentioned brushing
suppressed surges swelling rising tides of unslaked desire
sweet wet spillage sliding into sublime simpering
sip slow sultry summer evening simmering
interweaving sun kissed limbs glistening
blush of first touching over crushed
ice melting point hot steam rising
off sizzling surfaces sucking
on ambrosial lusciousness
moist pout testing
the rigid
edges
over
soft
biting
fruit
burst
stirred
thirst
nipped
in the
bud
short
sharp
gasp
and i die a little

Nang Ta-khian murmurs to me

carve your name into my skin
i won't flinch
if you go deep
lie beneath me and make love
to someone else
i will hold you while you sleep

i don't mind you dancing
on my toes
swaying gently with my groans
know that i'll
stand by you still
bow and bend me to your will

and when you're old
but not as old as me
lean your back against my side
i will eat you
while
you lie

we'll be married in the spring
when you burst out of my skin
a leaf-bud un-
furling in the sun
or some such
precious thing

darkness

            shape-   shambling
    up   late-   shift   str   eets
  slanting   through   one-eyed   wind   ows
  spilling   out   of ran   sacked   cupboards
  seeping   into   slink   ing   fissures
  filling   up emp   tied   vessels
   peering out   of   hollow   -throated   drains
   craning round   draught-   shrouded   doors
    swallowing   whole rooms   in a single   gulp
     creeping   off clinging   floors
      slipping   round   an ankle
       folding   over   a rib
       insinuating   into   a chest
         to rest,   gaze   up at you
            out of   your   own
              flutt   ering
                  heart

Portrait of a woman walking home

"Every breath you take and every move you make
Every bond you break, every step you take, I'll be watching you"

— Sting

I like the way the sinking sun slips a golden aureole around you on that last straight stretch
of twilit street just before you round the corner falling suddenly under the towering
penumbra of these deserted edifices so recently bustling with workers exiting—
their veins visibly throbbing with concerns of the day—now soaring in
silence stripped of activity as if subjected to the unexpected descent
of some cataclysmic event while you were finishing up that last
pile dropped off by your manager with such urgency it needed
completing before his return tomorrow morning and though
you held up your end now finding despite your own best
instincts you are wandering halo-less—alone—down this
dusk-lit street clutching your bag against a skateboarder
shooting out from under a gaping facade like that time
with the razor-blade-wielding trio you inexplicably
chased and though you escaped unharmed there
is always that scar of doubt lingering alongside
the stomach-churning whispers and worse—
the still-felt imprints—but there is no
escaping the current situation
and that really is such
a nice pair

black stockings
perfectly paired with
those moderate heels showing
off your finely toned calves your hem
gliding just above the delicately curved backs
of your knees stirring in unison with the soft waves
around your raised but ever-so-slight shoulders and you
know though you do your prescribed daily workout with
just enough resistance you will never quite muster the power
you would need and it takes a certain set of eyes to realise on
your approach through the now-profound dusk to the welcome
arc of each lamppost that your silky blouse illuminates so precisely
from behind one can pick out the exact lines of your body moving so
fluidly within its satiny folds sashaying with the swing of your hips though
I know you are making extreme efforts to lessen the sway there is a certain gait
you cannot ameliorate in this corporate get-up—skirt over heels over female pelvis
and it is so obviously more-than-a-little inadvisable for you to have placed yourself in
this delicate position where you might be seen to provoke a certain reaction in an onlooker
of a particular disposition—it being late and you quite clearly under-dressed for the hour and
with every breath you take wondering why it is
ourselves like this
we have to watch

for all the #MeToos

i can't help but   feel
there should
be a
#MeaCulpaToo

i see
so many men
patting   breast
pockets and
groping at   rear
view glasses

but of course
that would   take
a different
kind of courage

final offensive

the nuclear weapon
of the sexual predator
no-one will believe you

m is for monster

it took him a year
of persistent single assaults
topped by one allied attack
to teach her his place
for a woman, in a world of men

it took her a year
of consistent embattled defeats
capped by one crushing subjugation
to learn his place
for a woman, in a world of men

it took her one year more
of committed self-denial
to swallow the bitterest pill
—she couldn't shrink from this place
fully grown to a woman, in a world of men

in her midnight cries i learned their names
this monster and his minions
should i type them here so their mothers
and sisters can distinguish his place
for a woman, in a world of men?

and what's in their heads, these men—
as they let go their daughters
each day—do they pray
that someone won't show them his place
for a woman, in a world of men?

PLEASE DO NOT FEED THE ANIMALS

a colleague of mine once observed i have a mind
like a steel trap—it may have been meant
as a compliment but it didn't
feel like that at the time

        he was wrong of course it is much more like a labyrinth
        expertly appointed to hold within safe confines
        a variety of monsters of commonplace yet
        inexplicable design

spectres hermetically sealed in lightless
spaces where they pace un–
attended waiting
to be fed

        which i do periodically subconsciously—ignoring the signs and
        tripping that switch to wander into familiar habitats
        here the electrifying jolt of nightclub lights
        striking out of the demi-dark

there the fluorescent flicker of the too-bright doctors' rooms or the
overhead strip lights humming along with the rumble of
subway tracks a twilit street or the sunny playground
running-running from the old man coming

with his white-haired wreckage of sagging flesh hanging
from his open fly and i am eight years old again
and i can think of nothing else but *running*
and in that room there

is only running and running and in each other there are
the others—other things coming and then
there is the no-no
no

NO *NO!!* cell where the light is nothing but
subterranean murk the soundtrack
a thundering heartbeat above
oblivion

each time determined i will try something different but
it always ends the same so i lock the door again
praying one time the switch flicks
i will find the light

warmed to an early evening glow where there is nothing hungry waiting just a
tattered mound of dusty rags & a scattering of shattered twig-like things
only slightly too white—fragments crushed
between steel teeth

crush

"In 1910 Dr. Napoleone Burdizzo, an Italian veterinary surgeon, invented the instrument which carries his name... It is used to crush the spermatic cord within the scrotum, resulting in testicular atrophy within about 40 days."

— Robert Zufall, "Use of Burdizzo Clamp to Crush Vas",
The Journal of Urology, vol 80, No 3, September 1958

i didn't want him
only crushed
that he would learn
the same stale breath
he had filled me with

killed
just enough
to exhale
of despair
over time

i used to
hark at the creak of the
door, shiver at
the straw
caught on

picture the scene
shed
the quiver of
shred
his roped shoulder

the spill of
eyes after
soft
warming the chill night
his shrivelling truths

light pricking
all that darkness a
whimper
air
laid bare

the truth is i just needed
to crush his tiny mind
too
at the time
easily

someone
but mine was
inconvenient a truth
too
brushed aside

unlike this
ear for all these
"no-one will believe you"
inconvenient truth
trumping

rancid exhalation in my
years
his
always
mine

last night i heard
creaks in the
shuffles of small feet
in a
a gaping grate

the sounds of
inconvenient
assembling

undeniable
dark
the smack of a stick
soft palm
of rusted metal

countless
truths
for a reckoning

in the name of the Almighty

clouds swarmed in great dark clumps
a malformed day transformed to murk
as she was dumped—a squall settling
beyond wailing walls, wind bawling

following through the icy halls
head bowed, bag in hand
flat soles slapping cold stone flags
and the flailing later

rain pelting the rattling panes
sleety pellets rat-tat-tattling
piercing rivulets streaking down
spittle sprayed in the face

a dark veil drawn
across her *devil's spawn*
born under a cloud
a storm in stained swaddling

this pink squirming sin
slight in the hand
delivered to darkness as the
paling face of day turned away

to a railing night
silent mite
dispatched before
he ever saw the light

Suffer   the little children

The last star   climbed the still-black night
Sha/dows creep/ing,   he app:eared
Lam/b/ent shaft   by   her side
Unholy wailing   un/leashed   under eaves

The first star   crossed the coming-night
Shadows rose:as   he declared
Take her now   be/fore it's light
Spit(e) searing   smoke- filled   air

No   bright-star   came   to guide
Shadows   scat/tered,   no shep/herd
On that   long   and   winding ride
Through   stinging sleet   un/heard

All the stars   had hid   their light
In shadowed gather/ing   he emerged
Bring-him-away-quick   devil's   blight
Looming ha/bits,   great   black   birds

Not-a-star   climbed   the heap/ed night
Shadows fall/ing   she   slipt-away
Child-mother   night-visited only-son sacrificed
Secret burdens   she would   bear   to the clay

A   lone star   skirred the   cloven night
Under- sha/dow   he was   dis: appeared
Swaddled tight   stones   piled high
Alone   to hold him   through the years

Until   the last star   breached the darkling brume
Between   gasps   came their cries
Shadows   passing   through-the-tomb
From which
          He'd rise

you have to be tough to be a man

there are things they don't tell you
when at nine or ten if you're lucky
a considerate mother or sister sits
you down to tell you
good girl and
how very lucky you are
that inside you is a miracle
of soft warm tender places
where if you're lucky oh so lucky
you can grow a small perfect child
from the tiniest seed
this very considerate mother or sister
omitting the bits about how
many times *good girl*
you will spread
your legs for foreign objects
to probe the miracle of your
soft warm tender places
how very very lucky
you'll be when a man you've
never met before tells you
good girl to
take off your panties
curl up in a ball
and face the wall
like a small unwilling child
so you can't see
when he shoves the sharp shock
of cold steel from behind inside
your soft warm tender places
the weight of him pressing
and breathless right
before he tells you good girl
                Take off your top and bra
and
                You have beautiful breasts
as *good girl* you stand before
him so he can examine

them first with his roving eyes
then with his tough manly hands
and though you are no longer
nine or ten sitting *good girl* with a very
considerate mother or sister
because politeness and your
teachings in life always guided you to
never be that small unwilling child
good girl you don't think to resist
until his smiling assistant *good girl* behind
his plush reception desk hands
you back your used card and revolt
crawls out of your *good girl*
soft warm tender places
but you're lucky oh so very very lucky
to be a woman because you have
to be tough to be a man
but women are formed
from goddesses' tears and
shards of splintering stars
under millennial layers
of immeasurable
downward pressure
in secret places
bubbling to thousands
of degrees of ancient
raging heat
before
erupting from the surface

Dear son

It's not about the trail of breadcrumbs
across the floor that I just vacuumed and washed
It's about respect
It's about being a woman
in a world where
my role includes
cleaning up after anyone who steps through my door
and many who don't
It's about being a chair
that anyone can sit on
without my say-so
No thank you
It is about
the greying men who
since I was thirteen
have seen fit to greet me with
their unwelcome tongues thrusting between
my unsuspecting lips
It is about not wanting
you to be that kind of man
when you grow up
So when I say
Get a plate
listen to me
asking you to be the kind of man
who treats a woman like an equal
or better still, like a queen
Like a crystal glass
to be handled delicately
with due deference
and only after permission is clearly granted
It is about
being the kind of man
who makes your Mama want to weep
with pride

If wallets were skirts

Sir, where exactly were you
when the *alleged* offence took place?
Ah, and would you agree—as outlined in earlier
expert testimony—that this is a *dark* street?
Thank you—and—were you *alone* at the time?
And—en route home—alone
via the aforementioned *dark* street—
where were you coming from?
I see. I believe
that is
a *drinking* establishment?
And were you *in company*
at this establishment?
I see. And sir—
can you please speak up for the benefit of the jury—
when you were *alone*
at this *drinking* establishment before you
wandered down the aforementioned
dark street in the company of
no-one, had you been *drinking*, sir?
Thank you. And if I might, sir,
could you please estimate
how many drinks
you had consumed
on your own at this premises?
Was this *your first time*
venturing out
drinking alone?
Would you care to describe to the court
what you were wearing
at the time
your wallet was allegedly stolen?

Still I rise

(After the incomparable Maya Angelou, 1928 – 2014)

You have stalked me down in city streets
with your grubby, prying eyes.
You have rubbed me with your smutty filth,
but still, like dust, I rise.

Did my sexiness arouse you
when I was barely aged thirteen
when you trailed me with your wanting
gobbing offers so obscene?

Just like storms and like winds,
sure as sunset and sunrise,
as the stars climb the night skies,
still, I'll rise.

When you followed me at eight
years old to display your naked crotch,
did my gaping mouth excite you?
Did you want to make me watch?

Does my indifference offend you—
doesn't make you quite so hard—
'cause I laugh like I've got diamonds
in my own precious heart?

You may slam me with your words;
you may strip me with your eyes;
you may score me with your coarseness;
but still, like your heat, I'll rise.

Does my derisiveness distress you?
Does it come as a surprise—
that I talk like I've got tactics
in the space behind my eyes?

Out of the sheds of men's shamefulness, I rise.
Up from an antiquity of blamefulness, I rise.
I am handed down from Amazons, baptised in their blood—
Daughter of Eve, I'd see you crawling in the mud.

Leaving behind nights of secrets and dread, I rise.
Into a daybreak that's flushed fulsome red, I rise.
Bringing the rage that my fine sisters gave,
I am the cry and the call of the brave.

I rise, I rise, I rise.

You'll never walk alone

The grandmother ever at my shoulder
What harm another little nub of butter?
A pinch of sage would lift the whole thing

Navigating the gaps as nimbly now as she did
In her dimly-lit kitchen with its three trip-up steps to sprinkle and stir
Her jealous Jack Russell and me always lapping at her feet

My grandfather appearing out of thin air, his fine white hair backlit
A smear of engine grease across his forehead
Cutting through the seasoned haze with its air of industry

My mother and her Irish twin hovering together
Inseparable after birth, throughout their lives
Between death and life, and forever after

Their baby sister borne between them
Whose tiny feet never touched the ground
For as long as they both had lived

In every sunset, a swell of light
To lift you away out of the falling day
And carry you through the dark

These ghosts I wear
Who bear
Me up

Fellow traveller

I see it in you
the shadow of that place
whose memory you cannot erase

There are others I know
I love, have loved
see in them no trace of it there

They are wide open
doors into rooms
with no empty chairs

No bags unpacked
from unplanned visits
to this landscape we'd rather not know

This country you get to
from over an ocean of
black broken glass

Whose language is silence
fished from the deepest abyss
echoed in shells washed up on a twilit shore

lapping to shadow
the shapings of faces
we have loved, ever love

these tracings you cannot erase
mementos of where
you get to from over

an ocean of black broken glass
whose language is silence
this nation whose border is loss

WRONG WAY
GO BACK

when we chased the train pulling out of the station
and you said *what the hell we'll drive there instead*
coasting coast to coast in one day, steady going
until we drove up that one-way road
the wrong way and you cracked
how friendly people were in this
midlands town—everyone hailing us
as you railed on through, shaking your blonde hair
and smiling your unshakeable smile, like that time
you sped through the red light on Sarsfield bridge
and waved your golden waves at the cop-car right
behind us, that miraculously never gave chase
then when we ran out of petrol on the way home
in the pitch-black back-hills, you cracked up
infecting me so entirely with your bonhomie
that we laughed all the way to help where you didn't
even have to ask the entranced farmer who drove us
back through the dark, all three of us crammed
in the cab of his tractor with a full jerrycan
to speed us singing *Westering Home* to our own coast
in our two-part harmony, yours always soaring to
my steady as she goes until your train
careened off the end of the track
and still every time I go back
driving home that lonesome road
between the black hills hearing your glorious
higher part stuck on repeat in my heart
loss spiralling into something
close to tear-streaked bliss
recalling you tossing
those platinum tresses
laughing all the way up
that wrong way
never guessing
we wouldn't
ever get to
go back

mutation

by early December
as Atlantic storms
battered the glass
in rattling attacks

and an odd
otherworldly fog
crept forward
across the harrowed sea

her shift was complete
she had slipped her
sloughed skin and dived
into the shimmering pool

of night

None shall sleep

I see the emptied cup
of a phantom moon
upturned in the mid blue
of a sunny late autumn
afternoon and I seek you there

I never did believe in our half-awake
half-asleep, that used up husk—
they burnt to the dulcet notes
of your beloved *Nessun Dorma*—
could have still contained you

Cold as ice pelting the panes
in stabbing sheets, chilling shrieks, riddle me this
the banshee queen could not name you, claim you
twisting the blade, took my head instead—
it was all that I could do to sustain you

Hearing the lilt of our own *Westering Home*
in between the keening bleeding through the cracks
I felt you rise over the ravening tide
leap across the void, lean into the wind
that gathered you up to carry you victorious

Your glorious emergence to where
your missing were waiting beyond my
howling your name drowning
in the blankets of your shed pain
to where I will follow when

My cup is fully emptied
and we will sleep no more

blue on white

there you are   smiling out   of a loop

love etched   so fluidly   in blue

in a passing phrase   *a dash of courage*

races over white   *hope,   dream,*   *desire*

silent strokes   daring to   *enquire?*

after all this   time   looped back over   four dimensions to two

time and you   folded in   unanswered

enveloped   in   hermetic   white

but for these   brief   resurrections

looping in   and   out of

fading   *b l u e*

Long distance

Sometimes
in that clear space waiting
as digits fly out in their
thin-air search

Did you get back safely?
You might ask
Have you eaten? Wear your warm coat.
There's a cold wind blowing and
they're saying there'll be snow in parts.

How's college?
You might ask
Will you be home for the summer?
We get so busy with the tour buses
stopping on their way up the coast.

How're the boys?
You might ask
When will you be home? Did Joe sleep through?
Any words yet? Would you ever think
of coming home for good?

Oh it's you love...
You might say
No word yet. Nothing showing up. Again.
But this pain won't go away.
I'm so afraid.

Did you get the flowers?
I might ask
Cerise pink, like your silk dress.
Joe's tiny fingers scattering scrunched-up
petals onto the ocean. Of this distant shore.

Did you get my message?
I might say
Can I take back. Every unkind word.
Every impatience. Un-presence. Every hurry-on.
Every tenderness misheard.

Joe turned ten yesterday.
I might say
Did they arrive? Perfumed pink drifting on helium wings
away into the clouds. Out of sight.
Somewhere in that blue sky

a call finds its answer
before I am told
This number has been disconnected.
Please check the number
and try again.

persimmon and rose

i see you
in each
sunset

as the fractious day
surrenders
to crepuscular
seduction

creeping rose
lusciously
unfolding
over-
ripe
persimmon
s
p
i
l
l
~ing
its
liquid
he(v)art

into the tumescent

s
u
r
g
e

of night's *fast* embr a c e

precious
seconds
lapsing

you are
again
i have
loved

and

gone

the sunset

al
-ways

Storms in teacups

The weather never got a look-in in my grandma's front room
windows veiled in mantillaed lace like the ladies' faces filing past

Weighing in for a gas after Sunday mass
brimming vessels spilling over, all drifts and domestic affairs

Elbows jabbing for a stir, sweetness rippling to the surface
lips testing the gilded edges, assembling to blow off steam

The canon's law rerun, expounded pound for pound
between ruddy-cheeked rounds, spitfuls spouted under full sail

Up and down the centre aisle—a duty bound for the new roof
a drip of rain echoing through the silence from the gallery

Jingling baskets passed around like the clinking cups filled
to their glistening rims, drained under raised eyebrows

and dipped chins until time and the tides of women find them run aground
capsized on a sidelined table, cupping each other's emptiness

Dust-dulled in their doldrums, their parched lips
long gone cold, all their stories told

I will arise and go

(After William Butler Yeats)

My people are a migrant clan
Prospering not by hook or crook or craft
But by diligent labour and an easy charm
Flung from one small corner
Across every wind-tossed sea
Mountaintop to valley floor
To lay a thousand roadways
Or stand on pavements grey
To explore wild tropical outposts
Hold fast to frozen plains

My people are an itinerant tribe
A heathen spirit tamed
Not by bonds or shackles or shekels
But by music and by elegant words
Though alongside our wanderlust
Cohabits a want in us—
That surges in each nomad breast—
To journey back again, top the last crest
To that first wide view
Across a childhood shore

To feel the heart leap
Like a salmon returned to familial waters
If only—in our dreams

"You're not from here?" [*politely]

i co-exist:
in the   nowhere   between green   green
green- fields   reined/rained/reigned with   grey
grey   grey- stone walls   falling down
to grey   stony   shores up
by the   grey   rolling ocean
only there
we   would call
it   the sea....   *-see*   see?

i co-exist:
in the   nowhere   between grey-   green
green   -grey trees   ceding/seeding
to grey   -brown wings   flash-
ing *fast* past   rumbling roads over   hot   dry   tracks
    confettied with   golden   starrrrs
only here
you   would call
them   st-aahhs....   *-arrrhs?*   ....aaaaaahhs.

i came from:
where   gossip leaned   across   long
brown   counters   lined with   brown
paper reams   for   wrap-
-ping *messages* and   tying
with pale   brown
string *(only there*
we   would call it   twine)
to the backs   of black
high bi-   cycles   squeaky-wheeling
through brown   muddy   ruts
down   holey/wholly/holy   country lanes
only there
we   would call
them   boithríns   *-botherings?*   boh-her-eeens.

i came to:
where   dragons   skitter across   sand-
stone   over-
                hangs   under
wide   out-reached   stands of
golden-brown boles   disrobing   in the white-
hot sun
and rainbow- feathered *arrows*
shriek through blue-blue-
blue- skies   where assassin   flies
spear bush   bees   right-
out of the   warm
swollen   air
only here
you   would call
it   aaay-aaaah...   -*aaay-aaarrrrhh?*   ....aaaaah!

i am: not *from-here,* no
-longer: *of* there
where i   come from   has
            disappeared
risen   into   the mists
that visit   the places   that
where i come from   had been
and where i   came to
        yet remain
herein   halfbeen halfbeing

i coexist:
in the   nowhere
                between

Three hours to midnight

A man jogs past with three dogs—
one carrying a frisbee,
one a crumpled bottle,
one a drooling grin.

A man and woman bear
an inflatable between them,
their toddler son trailing a cracked bucket—
a yellow spade dropped in his too-long shadow.

A man calls *"Lily!"*, loping
in the opposite direction,
returns with a crestfallen spaniel
straining against a red leash.

Winged will-o'-the-wisps
ghost across glinting pools,
archangels streaking over
seven shades of blue.

Teenagers test reflective depths
with a cast-off shred of fishing net;
sand martins swoop and call to cluster
in their nylon-lined cliff shelters.

A scorching orb slipping slowly
towards the waiting sea,
the burnished sand now cold underfoot,
neon bits drift over the tidal imprint

to catch in the pied tidemark
on this perfect evening after
another record-breaking day
towards the end of the earth.

transparency

a plastic water bottle
see-through debris
of an unplanned day-trip

its hollow clunk-clunk-clunk
into the recently emptied
recycling bin echoing through

the shallow chambers
of my heart—blood pulsing
into unwashed fingertips

the cheek-kiss of a too-warm
spring breeze—forewarning of
the oncoming storm

this knowing there is no right here
there can be no rights
out of all these wrong turns

what are we anyway
only ghosts living in
some future past

drifting blindly by
as Earth simmers
but persists

Recipe for a Giant Pickle

Take one shovel
A big, big   BIG   shovel

Dig one hole
A big, big   BLACK   hole

Extract all carbon in form of coal (approx 2.3 billion tonnes)
Reserve for later

Into the big, big   BIG   BLACK   hole, pour:
All rights of the Wangan, Jagalingou and Juru indigenous people

Slowly adding:
120 billion litres of groundwater (if available)
Futures of Carmichael, Thompson, Barcoo, Diamantina, Flinders, Bulloo
    and Warrego rivers

Stir well before adding:
Lake Buchanan, Lake Galilee, Betts Creek, and as many small aquifers of
Galilee and Great Artesian basins as you can get your hands on
(quantities subject to seasonal variation)

Slowly slide sand and soil of:
75,000 square kilometres of the Desert Uplands
into the big, big   BIG   BLACK   hole

Using a sharp-bladed mixer, carefully blend in:
Large quantities and varieties of unique fauna – particularly Black Throated Fi
(Add Wallum Frogs and Sugar Gliders for colour and sweetness)

Now add:
Over 14,000 species of irreplaceable indigenous flora – particularly rare boroi
(the rarer, the better)

Tip the remaining ingredients in and cover up:
23 laws relating to financial rectitude
Several large handfuls of environmental protection statutes

One billion dollars of Australian taxpayers' money
Sixty-nine thousand reef tourism jobs
(10,000 jobs should rise out of mixture to balance acidity)

You can now discard:
The strongly held opinions of 12 million Australians, as well as
Australia's international reputation

While you are waiting, take the 2.3 billion tonnes of carbon reserved earlier, and:
Slowly simmer one small blue planet

in a sunburnt country

here where men are busily at work
carving out new
deserts where wild
boronia once grew
rivers running rapidly
dry, wallum frogs croaking by
their thousands as sag-skinned cattle
carcasses graze on empty acres
fenced against an inland sea
one more migrant tide
repelled, kangaroo shot through
at sunset—their sorry hides
blanching over bleaching
bones for
daring to outrun
the culling gun
on
this new battlefront
where parched and starving natives
are run
aground swarming from
new deserts carved out
by men
busily at work where wild
boronia once grew
rivers running rapidly through
and wallum frogs once croaked
in their thousands

Drive-through nation

I have seen every articulation
of a kangaroo's form

An ageing   bloated   rear-end staring me down
legs splayed   from the parched margins

Stuck on the wrong side   a muscle-bound buck
caught in the averaged-speed rush of an oncoming freight truck

Crumpled heaps piling up between
skeletal trees and bleached-out fields

A sidelined juvenile   glazed-eyed   forefingers joined
in quiet supplication   to a silent sky

A crumpled mother   sickening wrench
tumbled young   flung from her emptied pouch

Swollen bellies   bulging eyes   stick legs
fenced in   edged out   run aground

I have seen every articulation
of a kangaroo's corpse

every one   a sucker punch
a carcass for each   solitary kilometre

four hundred and thirty-seven kays
past the turn-off for Jerrabomberra

and pondered the visceral
response of

my entitled life   gagging
behind glass on the unsmelt stench

The rotting bodies piling up by the
wayside of our stealing generations

Swarming clouds   collecting crimson tails across the
boundless plains   out here   in the dying light

THANK YOU FOR SHOPPING
WITH US

ITEM
250 G BEEF STEAKS *QTY 4 @

COST
15,455 LITRES OF WATER
26 KILOGRAMS OF
CARBON DIOXIDE
330 SQUARE METRES OF LAND
6.5 KILOGRAMS OF GRAIN

SUNDRY OTHER COSTS

DEFORESTATION (WEEKEND SPECIAL:
RAINFOREST GOING AT 1-2 ACRES
PER SECOND)

GREENHOUSE GAS EMISSIONS &
GLOBAL WARMING

LOSS OF BIODIVERSITY (SUNDAY
SPECIAL: ANIMALS & PLANTS GOING
AT 137 SPECIES PER DAY)

OVERUSE OF ANTIBIOTICS
(MIDNIGHT SPECIAL: LOSS OF
LIFE-SAVING DRUGS & GAIN
IN SUPERBUGS)

BRIBERY & CORRUPTION

GLUTTONY, OBESITY, CANCER &
HEART DISEASE

800 MILLION STARVING PEOPLE
(GRAIN FEEDING LIVESTOCK = FOOD
FOR 10 BILLION PEOPLE)

DROUGHTS & WATER SHORTAGES
(33% OFF WORLD WATER
CONSUMPTION)

LOSS OF LAND/LIVING AREAS
(45% OFF WORLD LAND MASS)

DESERTIFICATION

WATER POLLUTION
(DEOXYGENATION OF OCEANS
RESULTING IN DEAD ZONES)

TOTAL COST — INCALCULABLE

PLEASE KEEP THIS
RECEIPT AS PROOF OF
YOUR PURCHASE

bull market

it comes charging in ripping this arm right
off eyes wild and red with rage giant
ears flapping against its vast white
leathery hide like an over-priced
modern art replica made of patented
skins sewn together in patterned patches
painstakingly matched by nine year-old
boys with bleeding fingers sitting cross
hatched on warped boards knees
knocking elbows bumping in the
steamy dimness of some third world slum
nearby crypto-coin miners herding
mercurial figures ever onward and the nine
year-old girls already dispatched
to some seedier market misfortunate others
hobbled and sold for less than the price
of a return phonecall to a scam number
from your ivory tower mobile phone
trunk calling charging like a wounded bull
elephant eyes wild and red with rage giant
ears flapping against its vast white
leathery hide as it rips off my write
arm but no worries
i still have another
unlike my slum
sisters and
brothers

quiet unto the void

"There is, in every event, whether lived or told, always a hole or a gap, often more than one. If we allow ourselves to get caught in it, we find it opening onto a void that, once we have slipped into it, we can never escape."

BRIAN EVENSON, 'Fugue State'

no towering pyre is lit on which
will crackle bright against the pitch
the cracked and creaking broken bones
through silent night unbreached by moans

no gatherings of black-armed guards
no haggard hags in tattered rags
with gnashing teeth and wringing hands
no half-mast flags and martial bands

no vigils clasping candlelit
where mothers hold to clinging kids
no flowers piled upon a verge
by hush-filled mourners stiff as serge

no loyal hound morose and still
with hanging head will sit there till
beside no stone-marked burial mound
within no elm-lined hallowed ground

no golden light breaks through the clouds
no oils alight, no laying out of sacred shrouds
no vestal virgins swept along
in reverential dirgeful song

> *"Democracy is dead*
> *Vive la démocratie!"*

burnt offerings

swilling cinders
of eucalypt forests burning up
and down the coast
tinged with hints of fear
singed possum hairs lifting into
clear blue air
an earthquake in Italy shakes me awake
a mother crying somewhere
volcanic embers cycling into
smoke of broken promises
women's choices smouldering
charred remains of exiles' lives
democracy doused with lies
and set on fire
headless horsemen prancing in the coals
blackened souls stirring
soot from scorched relics
ashes to ashes

and my mother in a box too small
to hold her all
laid in a field with all the others
when she could have flown
with the four winds
so I could taste again
the sharp tang of her loss
married to the rest

lately everything tastes of ash

In limbo

A fighter falls to his knees—bloodied, all but broken.
A big man with small hands stands
stock still, unsullied.
Two lovers kiss, a humming bird
touches down on dust-palled ground.

Dragnet chases crisscross cityscape;
a dragged woman paces, hands on hips; coffee drips;
a shrieking toddler races.
Noodles drape wooden sticks like
wool unspooling from knitting needles.

A puffed-shut eye bleeding,
burning man reeling from a flame-swathed house.
Breathing in, breathing out—all around
a hundred heroes battle, hunger, thirst
—ordinary lives exalted

against a hundred unjust power-lusting
dusk-suited forms.
Pitch and thrust—
a blue-black plume;
one hundred, two hundred

souls rise and fall—
two hundred, three hundred years,
a myriad voices elevate the call,
Mozart burning bright—
a requiem—for good,

for the fall, for the rise.
One thousand, two thousand,
a distant age—whispers in a cave
fighting this one fight
for the throng, for the long run.

Two thousand, three thousand feet in the air,
hissing into demon-occupied night—
svelte armour beaming light—
an ice-tipped angel
carving wings.

Faces alight, three hundred hearts expand in darkness,
pale rose blooming
out of gloom as
CX303 hurtles towards
a Hong Kong dawn.

deliver us from evil

faces alight, heads bowed, kneeling
thumbing shining orbs from right to left
counting their blessings, prostrating
lamenting their losses, pleading

standing, ears burning for the words
spewing in unending streams
from the new pulpit
wild-eyed pontificates professing

the good, the bad, the immortal struggle
how to arm yourself for a shifting world order
where darkness gives way
to a pixellated light

a new religion for our children

after the commission

a waft of smouldering candle grease
laced with a trace of incense
the sharp slap of flat soles
on a marble floor
dark shapes filter past one by one
spectres reflecting on polished brass

Let us begin with a prayer
a rosary catches on a sharp edge
spilling shiny
Our Fathers, Hail Marys
and Glory Bes
between uneasy feet

doves cross to and fro
beyond yawning windows
a distant boom
silver tongues slick down old panes
glossing over transparency
light leaves the room

under the same clouds
a mother looking down
holds her dying son
the sodden air stirring
with a sudden chill
in some dark corner
a child is crying still

Leonora is grieving

They used to dig up shiny things in her back yard
Now they bury threadbare things there
Things that wore out long before they
dug their shallow furrows and
laid them down one by one
in their burnished chests
Things they let die
slowly
under the glaring sun
light leaching out of them
from holes worn by hopelessness
Holes you could see right through
Holes boring into you when you looked into them
Holes in their arms and stomachs
their legs and necks, a dark
hole where their
mouths
once talked
once smiled
Empty and silent
for the longest while
Holes they tried to fill in
with forgetting and shallow shiny sands
slipping through their hands
Like the red dust
spilling from
her cuts
to fill up
      another son's
              parted   lips

death in the city

on the rain-speckled edge
of an office-tower window-ledge
a kestrel guts a lorikeet
rainbow feathers twirling
through the grey city air
bemusing unwitting commuters
in their muted autumn suits
thirty floors
below

sideshow

an orangutan walks on two legs
wears a suit, learns a grimacing smile
to form words that make people
follow in awe and fanatic adulation

some mimic his words and use
them to perform inhuman acts
forgetting that an orangutan can
learn to walk and talk but that

does not make it human

in one hundred days

an old man
scrawls his name
and smiles

the earth
travels two hundred and fifty-seven million kilometres
three hundred billion stars go dark

a tiny cluster of cells
evolves into a fifteen kilo baby polar bear
one hundred and thirty-seven cubic kilometres of antarctic ice-caps melt

a royal empress tree
stretches four and a half metres higher
two thousand four hundred animal species die out

my sons grow two centimetres taller
almost one million children perish from hunger
an eight-year-old American girl is killed by a US airstrike

an old man scrawls his name
seventy-nine times
and smiles

Metaphoric fall

A sequel to 'Metaphoric rise' – a brief history of incidents
surrounding the 45th American Presidency

SABRE RATTLING

brazen hide blanching
in the white-hot glare
the paper tiger blows with the wind

COCKFIGHT ON THE PACIFIC

puffing up their plumage
two noisy minahs crow
over a torn white dove

STORMY DAYS

darting here, scurrying there
the old fox digs new holes
before the coming surge

ALL AROUND THE TOP-END OF TOWN

dodging writs of feasance
taxing times are weighing him down
pop! goes the weasel

The emperor's new nose

"Just one piece—they will never notice."
"No, it was not I who cut the nose from Lincoln's face," he proclaimed,
As he secreted the piece in his pocket just before
He ordered the summary evisceration of his predecessor.

"It was not I," he professed as black letters slicked their greasy trail,
Paving the way for war pipes to rumble over ancient bones turning
    in their sacred graves;
Erected a golden fountain to celebrate his glorious godhead;
Released a blue bird to spread his substitute truths far and wide.

Black letters streaking as he sentenced countless faceless women to
    untimely deaths;
Banished exiles, rattled sabres with foreign rulers, gagged scientists,
    dismantled archives, scorched the harried earth anew;
Reinstated dungeons to reinforce his rule.
But little birds carrying older truths rose up into the darkening skies—

Dodging bullets shot by his minion millions, still they came in their
    hopeful pink flocks—
Until he ordered every man, woman and child to beat great empty oil drums,
And one by one, famished and exhausted, the little birds fell from the sky.
Yet a single pink canary survived, which he plucked mid-flight,
    stuffed into his voracious mouth and smiled his victorious smile.

"The people are hungry my Lord." *"Let them feast upon my bread!"*
He declared, handing the peon a giant slice of empty air—
Which would be instantaneously replicated throughout the walled borders
Of his vast domain

"Just one more piece—they will never notice,"
He told himself as he reached
To snatch the last star from the ravaged sky
And gorge upon its fire.

fuzzy borders

i couldn't kill
a chicken   but i cook
its limp pallid
limbs   draped in pliant
translucent skin   chill
from the fridge   i couldn't

    kill   a chicken
    but i know i can   kill
    a fish—evil though it feels
    to pull   a flash of silver
    from the shimmering ocean
    the sinewy   tear   of flesh

around the   mouth
as i rip out   the hook
tipping it into   a box
to madly flap   then flop
drowning   in our element
or worse   still

    the sick hit of a stick   or quick
    slit of a blade   through   a
    pulsing underbelly, the spill
    of   slippery viscera
    it doesn't   feel   good
    to kill   a living thing
    i couldn't kill

a chicken though   i know
i can kill a fish, but my mind
runs wild   at the thought of
knowingly killing   a   child
a small, smiling,   shrieking
bubbling bundle   of unearned trust

ach   -ingly   slowly   slain
for failing   to fall   from the sky
behind   the   'right'   lines
and who decides   how   many
and when   and where   and why
while we   are   all

the monsters   watching
from behind glass   eyes
as one   after one
they are strung   up
by   so many   lengths
of slick   red   tape

the scattering

defaced pages   ripped
    from a family   scrapbook
      papers not in order
         dislodged leaves

    scattered   on the   breeze

          sister, brother and one other

      still unfolding in the mother

             a short story barely begun
     a father creased and worn

    tattered epic torn
       a sad symphony drawn
           from ragged notes
   folklore recycled
       over and over in
          candlelit sanctuaries
     where happier stories
        nestled between soft covers
           once upon a time

danger in low-lying areas

for months i watched
blue light in the darkness
small minds spill out small words
small hands spread and reach
to bend, warp, break
all that could be, should be great

for days i passed
the black screen
berating and blaming
the mass-entertaining
hooked on a loop, counting down
to more incoming footage

and here now in the grey light
comes the dawning
what if we are not seeking ruin
but searching the ruins
for a hand
battered and bruised

broad-backed, mud-slicked
bent but unbroken
reaching out of the mire
to catch a pale light
against the still
dark sky

Lament for Aleppo

Even the buildings, beat and bent,
Have given up their allied front—

All the facades have fallen in
To crumpled spines and shattered shins;

Their broken ribs have been disrobed,
Leaning in to woes exposed—

That no father will find safe return
To rest from decent labour done;

No bread be broken, table laid;
No child delight in stories shared;

No mother kiss a sun-blessed cheek
And lay her down to easy sleep.

No-one will mark this story down
As evil vanquished, justice done—

No innocents saved, redress remiss.
No honest record will find any good in this.

Even the walls seem moved today
Though still they stand in their silent array.

Breaking winter's spell

Did snowdrops nod their lazy heads
Cowbells clang across the miles
Milky droplets fall to earth
Spring rains soak the path beside you
Searchers calling, calling, fail
Till the snows piled high and wide
Seven children waiting, wailing
Scattered, seven paths diverged
While you lingered side by side

Marceline, the youngest nodding
Dreaming as the years piled high
High as mountains coated deeply
Pockets filled with snow and ice
Far from news of marching armies
Shifting borders, storming skies
All the world kept to its stride
While you lay in feathered billows
Still, together side by side

Marceline alone had scouted
Past the clanging cowbells swinging
Yearly, spring rains soaked her path
Now she sits snow-headed nodding
Hope as white as snowdrops blooming
Through the years had been her guide
Till the glacier slowly thawing
Gave her back her Mam and Papa
Found together side by side

Category four

We emerged blinking in the grey light
two small children clutched tight
amongst our gathered up blankets
rumpled from a fitful sleep
still clinging with a drift of fear

Like zombies after the apocalypse
stumbling with the others from the shelter
which had held to its promise
and withstood the wild hammering
that had nailed us to our allocated
strip of floorboards all night
and into next day
until the way was cleared

Passing a palm tree stretching out of sight
no sign of its base
jagged splinters hiding its years
testifying to the sweeping judgment that had
delivered itself in darkness
taking one, leaving its neighbour
A ragged path we followed
on our journey home
shivering over ripped off rooves
and warped steel where plate glass should have been
A mermaid missing in the bay
two now perched in place of three

I had ventured out only once
past security to hover uncertainly
at a balcony on the lee side
A brief let-up in restrictions with strict instructions
not to wander off; the calm would pass suddenly
I'd stood spellbound, not far past the witching hour
lingering just long enough to puzzle over
a cluster of birds improbably
huddled on an outside eave

It was only in the wake of Irma
that the answer came
They were carried with the storm
for hundreds of miles
held within the eye
surviving
for as long as they could fly

For a short time
we shared
that same space

nocturne in me

in the midnight hours
my uterus aches for truth

was it for this
it groans
i grew you
two fine children
for this planet gone mad?

swaddled them
in a saline bubble
that you could
cast them out
into a world at sea?

nourished them
with my pulsing blood
for you to
expulse them
from womb to bleeding tomb?

in the midnight hours
i feel a shrivelling inside of me

one fine day

a heady stir of musky earth
moist heat rising after early summer rain

the live heart of a scarlet leaf
islanded by dying edges

nectar-laden bush bees
droning between sun-warm crocus

a swell of purple blossoms against cerulean sky
jacaranda carpet underfoot

the citrus swirl of myrtle
spurred by a scattering of brush turkeys

a chorus of lovesick cicadas
drowning out the traffic background

the sun oozing ripe persimmon as it sets on
another hottest day on record

the sound of metal striking metal
inside my head

cup in hand

I:

i am pink and brown and green
white slicked with red
small belly swelling
with a welling glow
fresh, shiny, new
an empty cup
raised up, beheld

delicate as eggshell
a precious package
wrapped, unwrapped
filled and held
gently handled
warmth breathed
into a tender shell

II:

i am flush and
i am burgeoning
a rush of fulsome
flavouring
i am bergamot scented
apple chai cinnamon
twisted swizzle sticks

sizzling over subzero
chinks
i am fire on ice
sugar and spice
hold the lemon slice
i am all sweetness
and warm golden light

III:

i am a hollow cup
aching to be full
sting of hot spout
liquid rush
eager lips to suck
yearning hands to grip me
drinking deep

open mouthed
sighs into steaminess
spilling words
glorious gush
a honey of sweet nothings
emptied
i am nothing

IV:

nothing but thirsting
fill me up with lies
luscious streams
reams of untruths
tell me i am fineboned, beautiful
i have poise
overflow me with your guise

i am an ocean in a teacup
a torrent of want
storms raging in fine china
i am pink and brown and green
white traced with red
flash of gold
i am empty, used-up, cold

V:

an echo in space
waiting for purpose
desperately seeking rightness
i am a willing vessel
able now to hold
ready to bear secrets
brimming with expectancy

miracle filled
water spilled
running into red
hot comfort over
white dripping milk
cradling this new truth
overflowing the edge

VI:

i am bearer in arms
deliverer of charms
i am reader of palms
speaker of psalms
giver of alms
bringer of balms
creator of calm

bring me
your body broken
dewdrop of blood
your battered soul
bow down your head
i will make you whole
lip to lip
let me fill you up

VII:

i am cream slowly turning
in a late summer jug
yellow creeping in
no longer game for mugs
no more glazed over
perfectly reflecting
an outward world

i am pink and yellow, brown and green
white traced with red
an interior lattice
laid out in cracks
chipped, fractured, chinked
unworthy vessel
from which no-one drinks

VIII:

forgotten fragment
shard of a lifespan
i'm a puzzle of
time-faded china
a multi-coloured piece
washed up on a
wave-worn beach

jetsam plucked
from the forsaken
remembrance thin as eggshell
the smallest drop of ocean
a minute grain of sand
this mystery held
within a greater hand

IX:

i am pink folding into yellow
brown giving way to green
red dissolving into white
i am golden
molten
light

spring tableau

nectar-drunk bush bees
drone amongst
sun-warm crocus

cheeks powdered
eyes round with desire
nuzzling between velvet folds

emerging buzzed and rumpled
pollen-laden legs dangling
in the perfumed air

an assassin fly spears
his mark mid-flight
ferrying him to the back fence

honey stripes quivering
in the spring sunlight
life draining quickly

the end justifying the means
rendering the scene
no less obscene

it is the last minute
of his last day
but he dies with

a belly full of nectar

scion

high on a branch
on a soaring crown
in a grove of trees between
sunbeam starburst leaves
that twists and turns
but goes nowhere

kookaburras canoodling
far above the middle of
everything that is all
cicadas calling to prayer
the crash of a branch
in the out there somewhere

a memory infused in cells
falling to earth
immersed engorged dispersed
echo of all that is everything
cycling through dirt to rise
to a branch on a soaring crown

in a grove of trees somewhere
in the
out
there

in their scores, by sixes and sevens

a reverse   constellation
    an un-   *Milky*   Way
       backlights   the day
         black—pointillist—pirouette
            perpetual-motion ink-strokes
              dissolve   into   silvery   grey

                    el   *em*   *en*   *dash*
                     stream   volley   *vee*
               cee   *es*   surge   rush
             ripple   roll   swoop
            open—bracket/close—bracket
        swoosh   curve   loop
       ampersand   arcing   *allez-oop*

     allégro   *adagio*   *brisé volé*
    x   &   y   aband-   oned
  in   un-   random   feint   ballet
    as   a   thousand   clustered   star
        -lings   salute
            the   dwindling   day

whisperings

for Joe

i caught a windblown secret beneath a singing yew
i got it from a blade of grass who plucked it from the dew

the dew had heard it whispered amongst the sighing boughs
they'd slipped it from the passing breeze without the whys or hows

the breeze himself had coaxed it from a currawong on the wing
her sister on a branch one day let slip this little thing

she'd overheard it from a rock within the babbling brook
who couldn't keep it to herself this news that she had took

one moonlit night along her banks was where she'd picked it up
a thirsty little bandicoot exchanged it for a sup

the bandicoot was unaware how precious was this nub
she'd pried by dark from Mother Earth while digging for a grub

but though i call it secret, it's a thing that you once knew
you had it when you fell to earth—small, naked, nameless you

before you learned of worldly things and how to busy-bee
you held within your tiny heart the secrets of the trees

to be at once within & outside of oneself

as a bird takes in the sky
as the earth sustains a body
as a cup holds its contents
as a tree releases its leaf
as a speck drifts in space
as the shore receives the ocean
as feet wear a path
as a heart carries love
as light cedes to darkness

as darkness cedes to light
as love carries a heart
as a path wears feet
as the ocean receives the shore
as space drifts in a speck
as a leaf releases its tree
as its contents hold a cup
as a body sustains the earth
as the sky takes in a bird

take this cup

this g[u]ilded vessel
misshapen by its fulsome labours
these seams
warped and grimed with its passage
through time

these g[u]ilt-edged chips
chafed by the slippage of so many lips
this fractured glaze
with its sunbaked edges and its tannin
stain of age

take this cup
filled and lifted, emptied, washed up and
set out to dry
left on its shelf, past reflection but
into itself

take this cup
this miracle of daily work, that turned
water into blood
and with body broken
under stone interred

flesh will be
at last, made word

All Souls

A citrus swirl of myrtle crosses my path
as three skulking brush turkeys scatter dramatically
into the understory
Crushed sandstone scrapes under flagging sandals
blending with
the tick-tick distant and more insistent chitter and chirrup
perpetual Trisagion against
the far-off clamour of trucks and cars morphing
this second day of November into
the roll and thunder of mist-capped surf on distant shores

      And there's the sharp salt catch at the back of the palate
      My mother standing
      arms thrown out against the Atlantic's roar
      embracing the world with a desperate love
      like Jesus
      after the delivery of her death sentence
      and before her crucifixion
      Too far away too long ago
      but still the piercing and the gush of water
      The salt rub of old wounds crossing time and space

      The quick chirp
      of a message from my father
      eleven hours behind but instantaneously dispatching
      me to the fiery pits of hell where
      starched sisters must surely be burning
      Pharaohs in their hooded head-coverings shepherding
      the little children and their unmarried mothers
      through famishment into lightless catacombs
      saving an anointed few borne nameless
      in Moses baskets unto the Promised Land

A kookaburra laughing
carries me home through the clearing
where the wattles are bursting
their golden crowns dancing
against a brooding backdrop and
rainbow lorikeets will swoop
in later lifting our hearts
out of emptied cups and
away with them into
the heavens

Acknowledgments

My heartfelt, eternal gratitude to the amazing people who have supported and encouraged me to believe in my writing dreams – Jessie Lendennie and Siobhán Hutson at Salmon Poetry, my incredible husband and sons, my late mother, my father, Martin Doyle, Ciaran Carty, Ciara Kenny, Eleanor Hooker, Ali Whitelock, Michele Seminara, Peter Boyle, Maggie Smith, Anthony Lawrence, Hélène Cardona, Luka Bloom, Eddie Vega, Melinda Smith, Kerry Featherstone, Carol Rowntree-Jones, Wendy J Dunn, Philip Porter, Magi Gibson, Lliane Clarke, Felicity Plunkett, Magdalena Ball, Anne Elvey, Deborah Hart, Geraldine O'Kane, Colin Dardis, Christine Murray, Maria McManus, Jayant Kashyap, Nuala O'Connor, Lizz Murphy, Harry Hughes, Deirdre Vaughan, Tim Dennehy, Joan Thurecht, Anne Rynne, Shona Blake, Claire Watts, Kevin Bateman, Rochelle J Shapiro, Moya Pacey, Shane Strange, Paul Munden, Ken Casey, Amanda Eggleton, Natalie Fu, the entire Lonergan family and Judy O'Grady, to name but a few.

Thank you to everyone who has purchased, read, and taken the time to respond to my poetry, or indeed poetry anywhere.

Sincere thanks to the editors of the journals and other media in which work from this collection first appeared: *The Irish Times, Quiddity, Entropy, apt journal, FourXFour Journal* (Poetry Northern Ireland), *The Honest Ulsterman, The Canberra Times, Cordite, Verity La, Autonomy* anthology (New Binary Press 2018), *HCE Magazine, The Stony Thursday Book 2018, Stilts Journal, Barzakh* (University at Albany, State University of New York), *Women's National Book Association* (USA) *Sixth Annual Writing Contest Anthology 2018, DASH* (California State University), *signs* (the University of Canberra Vice-Chancellor's International Poetry Prize 2018 anthology), *hope for whole* anthology (Plumwood Mountain 2018), *Awake in the World* anthology (Riverfeet Press 2019), *Bangor Literary Journal, Live Encounters, The Poets' Republic, Burningword Journal, The Corrugated Wave, FemAsia Magazine, enthralled magazine, HUSK magazine, Pink Cover Zine, EMPWR, The Same, Not4U Zine, The Enchanting Verses, Panoply Literary Zine, Visual Verse: An Anthology of Art and Words, Bold + Italic, Poethead, HeadStuff, Burning House Press, Eureka Street, Bedford International Writing Competition Anthology 2017, Not Very Quiet Journal, In the News* anthology (The Poetry Box 2018), *LabelLit / Poetry Ireland Digi-M'App, The Remembered Arts Journal, An Áit Eile, Déraciné, The Monologue Adventure: Longings, Secrets, Triumphs* (2018), *Spirit of Nature* poetry and art exhibition at Manly Art Gallery in Sydney, *Australian Poetry Collaboration, Henry Lawson Verse & Short Story Competition 2018 Anthology, Black Bough Poetry* and *Scope magazine* (Fellowship of Australian Writers Queensland).

Special thanks are due to Jed Grainger at *The Corrugated Wave* for his layout design of the poem, 'Thank You for Shopping With Us', which is reproduced here with his permission.

My gratitude also to the Climate Guardians who performed 'Recipe for a Giant Pickle' at the *Biennale of Australian Art 2018*, the largest ever showcase of living Australian artists.

Sincere thanks to Cezary Korsieko, October 9 Arts, for permission to use his stunning 'Powder Flower' image on the cover of this book.

Notes on poems in this collection

'Out of a thousand cups' references the research by US physician, Duncan MacDougall who attempted to measure the weight of a human soul by calculating the mass lost by patients at the moment of death. Although largely regarded as flawed, the experiment popularised the concept that the human soul weighs twenty-one grams.

'Nang Ta-khian murmurs to me' draws its title and inspiration from the Thai legend of a female tree-spirit.

'In the name of the Almighty', 'Suffer the little children' and 'All Souls' remember the eight hundred infants whose remains were discovered in a septic tank on the grounds of the Tuam Mother and Babies Home in Ireland in 2017. Further information can be found in an article by the author of this collection entitled *Marked women, unmarked graves* which was published in *The Irish Times* in May 2018, available online.

'None shall sleep' derives its title from *Nessun Dorma*, an aria from the final act of Puccini's opera *Turandot*. A 'banshee' is the Irish for 'female fairy', a spirit said to herald the death of a family member by shrieking or wailing. *Westering Home* is a Scottish homecoming song written by Hugh S. Roberton in the 1920s and possibly derived from the Irish song *Trasna na dTonnta* meaning "Across the Waves".

'I will arise and go' derives its title and also draws on the lines "While I stand on the roadway, or on the pavements grey" from 'The Lake Isle of Innisfree' by William Butler Yeats.

'in a sunburnt country' derives its title from a phrase in the Dorothea Mackellar poem 'My Country.'

'In limbo' is a quasi-ekphrastic poem responding to the images on hundreds of screens in-flight while listening to Mozart requiems journeying between Ireland and Australia, the overriding image being the age-old battle between good and evil.

'quiet unto the void' is a mock-lament for the death of democracy – the French line to finish is a subtle dig at the heavy-handed response by the French Government in January 2019, cracking down on 'yellow shirt' anti-government protestors.

'Lament for Aleppo' was inspired by a news photo of a man smoking a cigarette, sitting on his bed in an upstairs room of a house, with half the walls missing, in the war-ravaged Syrian capital.

'Category four' is based on the poet's real-life experience of weathering through Tropical Cyclone (Hurricane) Ului in Queensland, Australia with her young family in 2010.

'Breaking winter's spell' remembers a couple whose bodies were found in the Swiss Alps in 2017, seventy-five years after they went missing. Their only surviving child had never given up hope of finding them. In folklore, the snowdrop is said to "break the spell of winter".

'Leonora is grieving' remembers a young man from the declining Australian outback mining town of Leonora, a victim of despair, spiralling into drug/alcohol abuse and, ultimately, suicide.

'in their scores, by sixes and sevens' references a study by Young GF, Scardovi L, Cavagna A, Giardina I and Leonard NE (2013) in "Starling Flock Networks Manage Uncertainty in Consensus at Low Cost" *PLOS Computational Biology Journal* which found that starlings interact in sixes or sevens to maintain complex flight patterns during murmurations.

'take this cup' is, in part (somewhat wryly), a response to the quote: "It's not the word made flesh we want in writing, in poetry and fiction, but the flesh made word" by William H Gass.

Originally from west Clare in Ireland, and living in Sydney, Australia, Anne Casey is an award-winning poet and writer. Over a 25-year career, she has worked as a journalist, magazine editor, media communications director and legal author. Anne is Senior Poetry Editor of *Other Terrain* and *Backstory* literary journals (Swinburne University, Melbourne). Her writing and poetry rank in *The Irish Times* newspaper's Most-Read.

She has won or been shortlisted for poetry prizes in Ireland, Northern Ireland, the USA, the UK, Canada and Australia – including the Henry Lawson Poetry Competition 2018 – *Traditional Verse* (Australia); the Women's National Book Association Poetry Competition 2018 (USA); Hennessy New Irish Writing 2015 and 2017 (Ireland); Cúirt International Poetry Prize 2017 (Ireland); Overton Poetry Prize 2019 (UK); Bedford International Writing Competition 2018 (UK); and the Fellowship of Australian Writers Queensland Literary Competition. She was longlisted for the University of Canberra Vice-Chancellor's International Poetry Prize 2018.

Anne passionately believes that every poem, like all art, should leave you changed by the experience. Her poems feature internationally in newspapers, magazines, journals, anthologies, broadcasts, podcasts, music albums, stage shows and art exhibitions – *Quiddity, Entropy, The Irish Times, The Canberra Times, apt, Cordite, The Murmur House, Papaya Press, Eureka Street, The Incubator, FourXFour* (Poetry Northern Ireland), *The Honest Ulsterman, Déraciné, The Stony Thursday Book, The Australian Poetry Collaboration, Into The Void Magazine, ROPES, Autonomy* anthology, *Plumwood Mountain, Abridged, Verity La, The Monologue Adventure,* the *Poetry Pharmacy, The Poets' Republic* and Burning House Press among others. She is author of *where the lost things go* (Salmon Poetry 2017, 2nd ed 2018).

Anne holds a Law Degree from University College Dublin and qualifications in Media Communications.

Website: anne-casey.com   Twitter: @1annecasey

salmonpoetry

Cliffs of Moher, County Clare, Ireland

"Like the sea-run Steelhead salmon that thrashes
upstream to its spawning ground, then instead of dying,
returns to the sea – Salmon Poetry Press brings precious
cargo to both Ireland and America in the poetry it
publishes, then carries that select work to its readership
against incalculable odds."

TESS GALLAGHER

The Salmon Bookshop
& Literary Centre

Ennistymon, County Clare, Ireland